Clues to American Dress

Also in this series:

Clues to American Architecture
*by Marilyn W. Klein, David P. Fogle,
and Wolcott B. Etienne*

Clues to American Dance
by Carol Roan and Ann Gross

Clues to American Furniture
by Jean Taylor Federico and Judith Curcio

Clues to American Music
by Monroe Levin

Clues to American Sculpture
*by Kathleen Sinclair Wood
and Margo Pautler Klass*

CLUES
to
American
Dress

By E.F. Hartley
Illustrated by Jonel Becker Sofian

STARRHILL PRESS
Washington, D.C.

Published by Starrhill Press
P.O. Box 21038
Washington, DC 20009-0538
(202) 387-9805

ISBN 0-913515-63-9
Printed in the United States of America

1994 1995 1996 1997 1998 1999 2000 2001   8 7 6 5 4 3 2 1

INTRODUCTION 6

THE COLONIAL PERIOD 1600-1775 8

THE NEW REPUBLIC 1775-1860 24

COMING OF AGE 1860-1940 37

MODERN TIMES 1940-1990 54

SOURCES 66

SUGGESTED READING 67

GLOSSARY 68

INDEX 71

FASHIONABLE REMARKS 72

One of the first questions that enters a woman's mind as she thinks about an upcoming social event, job interview, or other special occasion is "What am I going to wear?" This question, while it may have always been important to women, has a different significance today than it did in the past, when limitations of wardrobe size and social or economic class placed major constraints on a decision modern women make with relative freedom.

Because the United States began as a series of colonies settled under the predominant influence of the British, the colonists clung for some time to British clothing styles. Before the American Revolution, dress was based on fashions worn by the wealthy and powerful in London, simplified and amended to serve colonial needs and conditions. Until the late 19th century, a woman was legally dependent on her father or husband, and how she dressed reflected his circumstances. Even for the wealthy a woman's lot was hard. It entailed (in addition to making clothing) bearing and rearing children, seeing to endless household tasks, and nursing her own family as well as relatives, friends, and neighbors in times of sickness.

The Revolutionary War divorced the United States from Britain politically and economically, and the Industrial Revolution changed clothing manufacture from a cottage to a major industry. The development of powered machinery enabled a greater variety of goods to be produced quickly, cheaply, and in abundance. Mass-produced, ready-to-wear clothing, as well as labor-saving devices for the home, alleviated some of the burden on the housewife and gave her some time for leisure activities.

The end of the 19th century saw the rise of women's rights which opened the way to greater freedom from traditional burdens, and clothing reflected the change. Today, while designers offer new ideas, comfort and price are additional factors to be considered, and it is almost impossible to pinpoint economic, religious, or ethnic background solely from what a woman wears.

What is called "high fashion" usually goes to extremes. Fashion has emphasized different parts of the body at different times, selectively revealing or concealing according to popular trends. Wasp waists emphasize breasts and hips, loose garments show movement of the body beneath, and short skirts draw attention to legs. Throughout history, women have tried to adapt their own shapes and sizes to current fashion, no matter how unrealistic this might be. Fashion plates once represented the ideal, but this was generally as far from what women actually wore as today's models in glossy fashion magazines are from what most of us really look like and the clothes we wear. The main difference between fashion and dress is that fashion is revolutionary while dress is evolutionary. Fashion has always been in the forefront of social change, and in general women pay some attention to it. In practice however, when new ideas are presented, one style melts gradually into another and people update their wardrobes accordingly.

The story of what American women have worn over almost four centuries must be considered in the context of the times in which the women lived and the lives they led. In spite of the vagaries of fashion, clothing in the United States has always reflected the general lifestyle of its wearers. Over the years, trendsetters constantly introduce new ideas; shapes and styles change constantly, yet most women remain more concerned with availability and suitability than fashion.

This book does not attempt to catalogue every tiny fad in the history of American female dress, but rather to provide an overview of the main trends, although some details are too interesting to omit.

The earliest successful British colonists in the New World were Puritan in the north and non-Puritan in the south. Religious beliefs, class structure (based on English social and economic divisions) and, ultimately, climate, contributed to the difference in clothing worn by women in the two areas. By the end of the 17th century, religious influence had abated but class difference was still firmly defined.

A common denominator to women's dress everywhere was the shift, also known as a smock or chemise. This all-purpose, loose undergarment reached to the knees, had full, elbow-length sleeves, and a drawstring neckline to facilitate breast-feeding. The upper classes' were made of fine linen or silk, while lower class women used coarser materials.

Chemise, the undergarment of the 17th and 18th centuries.

Gowns had bodices that laced at the front or sides and, for rich women, skirts that reached to the ground. Poor women's skirts usually ended at mid-calf.

Face mask to protect complexion, late 17th century.

Women of the upper classes everywhere protected their complexions from the elements with masks made of velvet in winter and silk in summer. These masks covered the entire face and were held in place by a button clenched between the teeth or attached by strings tied around the head. The Southern upper classes wore lace caps over curled and ringleted hairdos, while in the north, the hair was almost completely invisible. Laborer's simple hair styles were covered with caps or kerchiefs.

Muffs made of fur or cloth kept hands warm in cold weather, and gloves were worn in all seasons. For the gentry, gloves were made of fine leather and often were embroidered. The poor knitted gloves to meet their needs.

Elizabethan style from England, ca. 1600.

Silk or cotton stockings were worn by the rich; few of the poor owned them. Shoes for ladies were dainty and high heeled, while the few laborers who had them wore home-cobbled versions of rough leather.

Jamestown, the first successful English colony, was founded in Virginia in 1607. Settlers here were often of the upper class and minor aristocracy in England, and they imported black slaves from Africa and indentured servants from England to labor in plantation fields.

Two very different clothing styles were worn by women from the ruling and laboring classes. Upper-class women wore clothes with a decidedly Elizabethan look: gowns with small ruffs at the neck, long sleeves with slight puffs at the shoulders, and full skirts held away from the body by a sausagelike cushion called a farthingale, worn just below the waistline. For the upper class, there were no strictures as to colors or trimmings, but complaints arose when a Jamestown cow-keeper went to church in "fresh flaming silk," a

Pocahontas in beaver hat and lace ruff, 1616.

fabric considered above her station. In contrast to the Puritans of New England, southern ladies delighted in ribbons, laces, embroidery, jewelry, and cosmetics. A portrait of the Native American princess Pocahontas, painted in 1616 while she was in London, shows her dressed as an upper-class Englishwoman with a beaver hat, lace ruff, red overdress, and black underdress, all similar to what a white upper-class settler would have worn. A 1622 woodcut illustration of an Indian attack on a farm near Jamestown pictures the women in simple, high-necked, long-sleeved bodices, long skirts, caps, and aprons; showing what was worn by lower-class women.

The Massachusetts Bay Colony was founded in the early 1600s by Puritans, protestors against what they considered to be the pomp and vanity of the establishment in England. Primarily farmers, they were a stern and uncompromising people, and their clothing was utilitarian rather than decorative. In form, it was much the same as England's, only much more conservative.

Women wore an overskirt that could be looped up to keep it out of the dust or mud, and a high-necked, long-sleeved jacket with a wide, white linen shawl collar. They pinned up their long hair and always wore caps that concealed it completely. Thick wool stock-

Working-class outfit from Jamestown settlement, ca. 1620.

ings, secured above the knee by garters made of thin strips of cloth, and square-toed leather shoes with low, wooden heels completed the costume. Plain, untrimmed aprons were always worn both indoors and out. In inclement weather, a wool cape covered the outfit, and a tall, conical felt hat with a wide brim was worn over the cap. Garments were fastened with lacing, buttons, or hooks and eyes. Durability and service-ability of clothing were the primary considerations.

For Puritans, any hint of sexuality was strictly forbidden. As late as 1651, the court of the Massachusetts Bay Colony issued an order giving town selectmen the task of deciding if people were dressing illegally above their rank. Fifteen years earlier, a law had been passed ordering that "no garment shall be made with short sleeves, whereby the

Puritan dress, ca. 1640.

nakedness of the arm may be discovered." Anything that even remotely hinted at sensuality, including loose, flowing hair, curls, jewelry, lace, ribbon trimmings, fancy hats, luxurious materials and, of course, cosmetics, was strictly forbidden. Although other groups settled in New England, the Puritan influence was strongest, and women's clothing followed English styles.

It is a common misconception that Puritans wore only black or gray. Black, considered a "strong" color, was consigned to leaders.

Ordinary folk wore what were called "sadd" colors: reds, purples, oranges, browns, and various shades of green, all obtained from natural dyes. They were muddy and earthy, rather than brilliant shades.

In the early 1600s, fabric for clothes had to be imported, usually from England, to be made up at home, as there were no dress shops. Flax was produced in quantity in New England in the 1640s, and sheep provided local wool. Housewives often spun thread and wove their own cloth, usually linsey-woolsey, a combination of woolen weft on a linen warp, coloring it with dyes extracted from barks, roots, flowers, or berries. This is what is generally referred to as "homespun" and was most often worn by the lower classes in all the colonies. Garments made of this fabric changed very little in appearance over the century. Other fabrics included kersey, a fine woolen cloth; fustian, a warp of linen and a woof of cotton; drugget, a twilled wool used for linings; and camlet, a blend of wool and silk or animal hair.

Upper-class women had their clothes made of imported fabrics by a seamstress at home. Some had clothing made in England, but achieving a proper fit could be a problem. Even the most affluent had a limited wardrobe. Newer clothes were reserved for Sunday worship or other special occasions, and brides wore their newest dresses; the white bridal gown is a 19th century innovation. When new garments were acquired, the former "Sunday best" became everyday wear. When a woman died, her clothing was distributed among relatives and friends.

Unfortunately, not much clothing has survived from this period. People wore their few garments until they were more than shabby. When edges frayed, seams split, and elbows worked their way through, clothes were darned or patched. When all else failed, the garment was cut down for children's wear. People seldom took baths, and infestations of lice and fleas were not unusual. Dry cleaning was not developed until the late 19th century. Clothes were laundered infrequently in boiling water with a strong lye soap, then dried in the sun and wind. There were no deodorants; sweat-stained, dirt-rotted fabrics became permeated with body odors. The Southern gentry used perfume lavishly to disguise the problem; Northerners evidently ignored it.

Toward the end of the 1600s, under the French-influenced King Charles II and with a release from Puritan rule, dress in England became more formal, and the southern colonies followed suit. Necklines plunged and breasts were pushed up by tight bodices. An overdress with full sleeves was pulled back to show an elaborate underdress. Hair was arranged in seemingly careless ringlets combined with long, corkscrew curls. Cosmetics and jewelry were also very much in evidence. The inventory of a wealthy Maryland lady who died in 1697 in-

Formal style of the Southern colonies, ca. 1670.

cluded rings and earrings set with precious stones. Prized pearls frequently passed down from generation to generation. Men owned everything, including their wives' personal effects, but they often bequeathed jewelry to their widows. During these years, New England women followed the new fashions with restraint; they continued to cover their bosoms, use only somber colors, and hide their hair under caps.

The Quakers, who established Pennsylvania in the mid-1600s, wore simplified versions of the current styles. They were not allowed to use prints or colors that were anything other than "grave" (gray or brown). Everything had to be "needful" (necessary) and anything that suggested "worldliness," including trimmings, was proscribed.

Spanish settlements in the West and in Florida and French settlements in Canada and Louisiana were, at first, largely military outposts with few female settlers. They had little impact on the eastern colonies, which were under British rule from Maine to South Carolina by 1700, although peopled with Dutch, French, German, Irish, and Scottish settlers, as well as African slaves. Native American women nearly everywhere were displaced; where they managed to stay, they were forced to assume a form of European dress.

Fashion doll, mid-1700s.

Immigrants constantly arrived from many European countries, but English influence was so widespread that all the women soon wore English-style clothing. Settlements that had been little more than villages grew into mercantile centers, where an urban lifestyle and middle class began to emerge. New settlers brought the latest London styles to these towns, and they were quickly adopted. "Fashion babies," dolls adorned in faithful replicas of current modes from undergarments to gowns, including the newest hairstyles and accessories, were eagerly welcomed. Dressmakers and milliners were kept busy creating outfits to order in the latest fashions, colors, and fabrics for their rich clients.

Petticoat with overskirt, ca. 1700–1710.

By 1700, women in the northern and southern colonies were wearing similar styles of clothing, with allowances for climatic differences and for the conservative influence of the Puritan religion in New England. Skirts had widened and the usual gown was, in effect, two sections, a bodice, often fitted with boned stays to make it smooth, and an attached overskirt that was drawn up on both sides to fall in graceful folds from the back of the waist over a separate underskirt of a contrasting color. This was called a petticoat until the 19th century, when that term came to be applied to lingerie. Necklines were low, cut square or oval. Under full, elbow-length sleeves, the lace or frilled edging of the shift could be seen. Undergarments were an integral part of the costume and were not considered sexually suggestive. Servants and slaves wore the shift as a blouse would be worn today. Ladies' hair was dressed with curls on top of the head and ringlets down the back. The commode, a tall, starched linen or stiffened silk headdress, was perched in front among the curls. Lower-class women continued to wear close-fitting caps. Shoes and stocking showed little change from those of the 17th century.

Commode, a starched headdress, ca. 1700.

Over the next 20 years, skirts became wider and pads were added at the hips. The overskirt might still be looped up but as often as not was allowed to fall freely from the stiffened bodice, which had lengthened to a point in front and was often decorated with bows. Necklines rose slightly and sleeves narrowed. The commode disappeared, and hair was dressed more closely to the head and usually surmounted by a cap.

Around 1720, a new dress style was introduced. It was referred to as the Watteau sacque (often anglicized to "sack"), from the late 17th-century French artist who painted

High neckline and narrow sleeves, ca. 1720–1740.

ladies in charming dishabille. At first the sacque was simply a loose overdress worn over an underskirt stiffened at the hem with a hoop. It soon attained a form that would remain in style for years: the overdress became formfitting once again, but from the back of the bodice at the shoulders, wide pleats or gathers fell to the floor.

Formfitting styles necessitated the use of corsets, which were worn over the shift but under the bodice. They were shaped like vests, higher at the back than front, with broad straps over the shoulders and tabs at the bottom to fit over the hips.

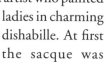

Watteau sacque, ca. 1740.

Made of closely stitched canvas and rein-forced with whalebone, metal, or cane strips, they replaced the stays that had previously been stitched into bodices. People continued to call them "stays" for nearly two centuries. They laced either in front or in back and often required help to pull them taut. From the time she was two or three years old, a girl wore stays, which restricted movement and

Reinforced canvas corset, ca. 1770.

maintained an erect posture, giving rise to the expression "strait laced." The corset must have been incredibly uncomfortable in hot weather and downright dangerous during pregnancy, but was accepted as a social necessity. It was used to mold bodies of all shapes and sizes to conform to current fashion, regardless of its effect on physical well-being. Medical wisdom of the period decreed that support was needed during pregnancy, but it is likely that many of the miscarriages and stillbirths of the age were direct results of corseting.

While the loose back lasted until the Revolution, the shape of the skirt changed. By 1740 it had become an oval supported by a hoop. Fullness at the hipline gradually increased, and in the 1750s a rigid framework was added. Made of bentwood or flexible wire, covered in cloth, and connected

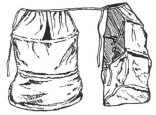

Panniers, used to create fullness at hipline, ca. 1750s.

by tapes, panniers (also called "false hips") attached at the waist and held the skirt out at right angles to the body. Women were forced to go through doors sideways until a system of hinges was devised that allowed the panniers to be folded up under the arms.

Overskirt and underdress covering panniers, mid-1700s.

Overdress and underskirt might be of the same or of contrasting material. Quilted, hand-sewn underskirts afforded a degree of warmth in winter. Bodices, while still cut low, were often worn with kerchiefs draped over the shoulders and bosom. For the lady of fashion, getting dressed was a time-consuming business that required the assistance of a maid. Women who were not so wealthy relied on daughters or members of their extended families for help. Most women wore simplified versions of current modes with modified hoops or panniers or, in the case of laborers, none at all.

Although skirts grew fuller, hairstyles remained fairly simple until the middle of the century. Caps trimmed with ribbons and bows were covered by broad-brimmed, shallow-crowned hats that tied under the chin. Capes made of wool, often trimmed in fur, were worn outdoors, and probably inside as well during harsh winters throughout the colonies.

Most footwear was leather with low, wooden heels, decorated with buckles, although well-to-do women wore high-heeled silk or satin shoes for

Broad-brimmed hat, mid-1700s.

special occasions. It was not until about 1800 that shoes differentiated between left and right feet, so 18th-century women probably had more than their share of foot discomfort and disability. In bad weather, women might wear pattens, a thick, wooded

Shoe, mid-1700s.

sole that was strapped to the shoe, or simple wooden clogs.

As the width of hoops and panniers began to wane in the 1760s, hairstyles became fancier. Even women in New England followed the trend of dressing the hair up from the face and piling it on top of the head, often with puffs and curls at the side and back. By 1773, hairdressing had become elaborate; ladies in Williamsburg, Vir-

Elaborate hairdressing, ca. 1770.

ginia, could avail themselves of the services of George Lafong, who offered "Headdresses so natural as not to be distinguished by the most curious Eye"—in other words, wigs. Those who preferred had their own hair dressed by a professional. These "heads" might stay in place for days, if not weeks, before being dismantled. They were built up on frames, supplemented with false switches, and glued together with a pomade or paste made of flour and water. Unhappily, weevils sometimes hatched from the flour.

The relief of undoing these things must have been tremendous. Caps became correspondingly larger. Full hairstyles spurred the development of something called the calash, a large, accordion-pleated bonnet stiffened to stand away from the head and protect the work of art beneath it.

By the time the American Revolution broke out, skirts had become shorter, often ankle length, and the sacque was beginning to disappear. While the overskirt and underskirt concept was retained, the top skirt was often puffed and caught up in several places. Hair continued to be powdered and dressed tall.

Calash, a pleated bonnet, ca. 1770.

For all but the most formal occasions it was covered with a cap that

Puffed top skirt, late 1700s.

was frilled around the face and often trimmed with lace. Most women wore aprons; delicate and lace-trimmed ones were more of a fashion statement than a necessity for the rich. Women who worked at never-ending household chores wore aprons made of sturdy homespun, coarse linen or serge.

Popular accessories included fans, which had a language all their own. Allowing a closed fan to touch the right cheek meant yes, the left cheek, no. Another favorite was a patch, or "beauty spot," intended to suggest a mole and to draw attention to a particular facial feature. In practice, it often disguised complexion blemishes. Smallpox left scars until inoculation was adopted late in the 18th century. Rouge and face powder were used, but not widely. Surviving recipe books give formulas for various beautifying lotions, salves, perfumes, and tooth powders, which were also available in shops. Dentifrices were considered beauty aids rather than necessities as people were reconciled to losing their teeth. Diet and dental hygiene were not connected in the public mind to healthy gums and teeth, and women accepted the old belief that a tooth was lost with each pregnancy.

Throughout the 18th century, short, choker-style necklaces were worn; sometimes a plain, narrow ribbon was tied in a bow at the back of the neck. Brooches were pinned to the center front of the bodice. Earrings were small. Little bunches of feathers of flowers were attached to powdered coiffures with jeweled pins or clips. Married women wore wedding bands, and portraits of affluent women show rings set with gems. Decorative shoe buckles might contain precious stones but more often were made of paste, or imitation jewels. Chatelaines, originally hooks or clasps worn at the waist to hold keys, now held sewing and other daily necessities. They might be made of chased silver or gold, but more likely of pinchbeck, an alloy of copper and zinc that looked like gold.

Trade with the Far East, especially India, introduced a new range of fabrics. Those that incorporated cotton, including calico, chintz, bombazine, muslin, and dimity, were best suited to the Southern colonies. These, as well as silks, satins, taffetas, and velvets, had to be imported and were extremely expensive. While a limited amount of Southern colonial cotton was absorbed domestically, most cotton dress materials came from Egypt or India. Contemporary accounts of fashions include mentions of lutestring, a soft silk, and padusoy, a smooth silk, both imported from Europe. A great variety of patterns (flowered, striped, spotted, and sprigged, to name a few) were available, as well as plain fabric in a large assortment of colors. Women decorated articles of apparel with intricate, time-consuming embroidery which must have caused terrific eyestrain, given the crude artificial lighting of the day.

Women of all classes everywhere tried as much as possible to dress like the wealthy fashion leaders, usually the wives of colonial governors and other prominent people. In 1763, Charles Carroll, Barrister, of Maryland, ordered clothing from his London agent for his bride, including: "one full Dressed Ladies Suit of Cloths of Rich white Ground Brocade if Can be got and fashionable with a slight Gold Sprig or flower interspersed / send in a yard of the same to spare."

Housewives in New England and on the frontier made home-spun for family use, and plantation mistresses oversaw the weaving by slaves of fabric to be sewn into shifts, bodices, skirts, aprons, and caps for the workers. Journal notices of runaway slaves or indentured servants often included descriptions of clothing. Servants frequently wore castoffs and occasionally helped themselves to expensive apparel before decamping. Mary Holland of Georgia, described by her master as "much conceited in her beauty," was last seen wearing a reddish gown, green petticoat, and white flowered cap. She also carried with her a fine lawn apron and flowered handkerchief that belonged to her mistress.

A girl child was considered an incomplete woman; she was treated and dressed accordingly, a faithful miniature of her mother, and was tutored in household skills rather than in reading, writing, or calculating. All women, rich and poor, northern and southern, shared the common experiences of pregnancy, childbirth, and death. After marriage, a woman could expect frequent pregnancies and several miscarriages or stillbirths. As the pregnancy progressed, she was kept busy with chores and simply loosened the waistband of her skirt to accommodate her changing body. Death was a frequent visitor, claiming people of all ages and stations. Women prepared their dead for burial and dressed themselves in black for a period of mourning, if they could afford to. At the funeral, mourners wore black, even if it was only a token kerchief or veil.

Some clothing from this period has survived and may be seen in museums. Generally, existing articles are gowns or accessories treasured for their association with special occasions, and were almost invariably the property of wealthy women who replaced items before they wore out.

The Boston Tea Party of 1774 was the culmination of a series of protests against Britain's iron grip on the colonies. Women were urged to stop buying imported items that carried a duty, including most fabrics and fashion accessories. The result was an emphasis, advanced by Martha Washington, on homemade woolen and flax cloth.

For 20 years after the Revolutionary War, women's fashions changed slowly but perceptibly. Hoops and panniers disappeared completely. Skirts became slimmer and no longer divided in front to show an underskirt. These skirts were called "round gowns." A sash delineated the waist, and the bodice

Fichu of draped fabric, ca. 1790–1795.

of the dress, made of the same material as the skirt, featured a lowered neckline, often decorated with a scarf or fichu of soft, draped fabric. Sleeves were tighter and reached to the wrist. Hair had escaped from the rigidly constructed form, with a long curl customarily allowed to hang over one shoulder. Powder was still used occasionally for special events. Broad-brimmed hats were trimmed with ribbons to match the gown. Hats and parasols had by now replaced masks as complexion protectors, and a few ladies still discreetly applied cosmetics.

Round gown with sash, ca. 1780–1790.

Following the Revolution, American women began to switch allegiance from English to French styles, with politics playing a large role in the creation of the look that ushered in the 19th century. Not only did the French Revolution end the power of the French aristocracy, but with the adoption of a governmental structure based on ancient Greece and Rome, it brought into fashion an entirely new form of dress. Almost overnight, "classic" garments appeared; gossamer-thin fabrics fell in a straight line from just below the bust to the ground. A low, oval neckline and short sleeves that puffed at the shoulders characterized this radical departure from previous styles. Arm-length undersleeves occasionally were attached to the hem of the puffed sleeves. Another variation on the classical theme added a loose tunic that was worn over the dress. A short jacket might complement the outfit in cool weather, with a cape or shawl to protect the entire costume from the elements. By now, a large disparity had developed between day and evening wear, which was more elaborate and made of finer materials.

"Classic" garment, early 19th century.

Even underwear was affected by the change. A few young women discarded almost all of the traditional underclothing, but most women still wore stays, which by now had assumed a different shape. Contemporary drawings depict a longer garment than previous versions that covered the hips and went up in straight lines, pushing the breasts up. A special corset for pregnant women was available "to compress and reduce to the shape desired the natural prominence of the female figure in a state of fruitfulness." A chemise went on under the corset, and drawers began to become available, although they were not yet in general use.

Short curls, worn close to the head, replaced the earlier bouffant hairstyle, while bonnets tied under the chin succeeded the earlier wide hats. Matrons and older single women still wore caps, which had been abandoned by most young women. Soft slippers without heels replaced shoes, and silk stockings were embroidered or clocked, as women's means allowed. While these were generally the standards for upper-class urban women, the trickle-down principle did apply. The message of current fashion traveled slowly from city to frontier, constantly changing to meet

Corset covers hips and elevates breasts, ca. 1800.

different needs, but eventually reached women at all levels of economic and social status.

Bonnet tied under the chin, ca. 1815.

The high "empire" waistlines lasted nearly 40 years, but other dress features saw change within that time. When Napoleon proclaimed himself emperor of France in 1804, rich fabrics returned to favor, including satins and velvets. Turbans became a popular form of headgear, given

"Empire" waistline, ca. 1805–1810.

wide exposure by portraits of first lady Dolley Madison. Mrs. Madison also used rouge and powder, but cosmetics generally were used less than they had been a generation earlier.

A new morality arose that combined traditional modesty with a puritanical streak and advanced into what today would be called prudery. It was described then as "gentility" and arose out of the romantic movement, which glorified womanhood as pure, fragile, childlike, and unapproachable by mortal man. Correspondingly, clothing sought to disguise the female body and to deny natural bodily functions. Wide skirts, multiple petticoats, and collars that covered the bust remained features of popular dress through the next several decades. Pregnant women draped shawls over their bodies or went into hiding if they could afford it; being in the "delicate condition" was not considered genteel. Despite warnings from the medical profession (which had made something of a turnabout on this issue), many women laced their corsets even tighter during pregnancy. As a result, children were sometimes born disfigured, corset lines imprinted deeply in their flesh.

Between 1815 and 1840, several changes took place. In 1815, waistlines were still high, but the wider skirt often finished with a

High waistline with flounce, ca. 1815.

flounce at the hem. Within five years, the puffed sleeve had enlarged and lengthened, and it continued to grow during the late 1820s and the following decade into what was called a "leg of mutton." With larger sleeves came shawl-like collars that covered the top of the arms, fastened at the neck and extending almost to the waistline. Simultaneously, waistlines began to descend and skirts, now supported by many petticoats, widened out.

When the waistline settled down to where nature had always intended, tight lacing to emphasize it was resumed. Drawers, dignified by the name "pantalettes," came into general use. With hair now generally dressed away from the face, ringlets replaced tight curls as the primary style. Ornamental combs helped control the coiffeur. Wide shoulders brought wide hats, often elaborately decorated with plumes, flowers, and frills, and large caps that entirely covered the hair. Women continued to wear slippers rather than shoes. Bead necklaces, lockets on chains, and small earrings are seen in portraits of this time; cameo

Leg-of-mutton sleeves, ca. 1820–1840.

brooches were particularly popular with the "classic" style of dress. Some American women used cosmetics, but most were cautious; overly blooming cheeks were apt to cause snide comment.

By 1840, leg-of-mutton sleeves had disappeared, and women's shoulders returned to their natural shape. From this time until the Civil War, skirts became increasingly wider and were held out by an increasing number of ever stiffer petticoats (now relegated to the status of underwear). An outer petticoat made of crinoline—a stiff linen-and-horsehair fabric—gave skirts a bell-like appearance. In the early 1850s, Empress Eugenie of France

Skirt with bell-like appearance, ca. 1840–1845.

popularized the wired hoop, used to maintain the bell shape without the multiple layers of petticoats. It also afforded a sinuous, sensual sway to a woman's walk.

The hoop skirt, which required yards of material to cover, often created difficulties and danger for the woman who wore it. Because women could not sit in traditional armchairs, a new type with vestigial arms had to be designed. A narrow doorway might cause the

Wire hoop, 1857.

hoops to bend, exposing more leg than was considered decent, and being outside in strong wind was practically an invitation to disaster. Contemporary cartoonists had a field day with such embarrassing situations, but there was real danger involved. Women who ventured too close to an open fire might set their skirts ablaze, an accident which killed or seriously burned many women.

When the wired hoop was introduced, Amelia Bloomer, an early advocate of women's rights and simplicity in dress, devised a new costume for American women. She appeared in a short skirt worn over full, ankle-length pantaloons that were quickly christened "bloomers." Needless to say, the style was derided as unfeminine and never caught on. The bloomers did, however, surviving for many years as part of costumes worn for exercises and sports.

Women generally wore a simple chemise with little sleeves underneath their clothing. Corsets became shorter and lacing tighter to push the breasts up and out. Those who needed a little help in that area used "bust improvers," which could be anything from a row of frills sewn inside the bodice to pads inserted in special pockets in the corset. Underclothing was invariably white.

Dresses in the early 1840s were made with pointed bodices gathered into tucks, but a rounded waistline soon appeared. Often a skirt came equipped with two bodices, one for daytime and one for evening wear, and all types of fabric, from light taffeta and cotton to heavy velvet and wool, were employed. Sleeves, which were tight at first,

Amelia Bloomer costume, ca. 1850s.

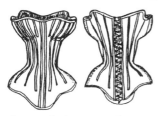

Corset pushes breasts up and out, ca. 1840s.

eventually widened and flared over undersleeves caught at the wrist. The arrival of the treadle-powered sewing machine greatly facilitated the creation of the yards of ruffles, flounces, and trimmings required by these developments. Stockings remained silk or cotton. Shoes, usually individually crafted by shoemakers, regained a slight heel. Outdoors, women wore elastic sided boots.

The popular hairstyle of the period, clusters of curls worn on either side of the face with a bun well above the nape of the neck, was replaced by a center part, from which the hair was drawn smooth, covering the ears and dressed to fall in a cascade of curls at the back. An easier alternative was to bundle the hair, always kept long, into a large hair-net, called a snood, at the back of the head.

Snood bundles hair at nape of neck, ca. 1860–1865.

The poke, a hat with a high crown and a deep brim that surrounded and projected forward over the face, held sway for years. At first large, it diminished over time and was eventually replaced among the fashion-conscious by a wide-brimmed hat with a shallow crown. Matrons and some single women wore caps at home, adding bonnets when going out.

Capes were succeeded by mantles or pelisses with sleeves.

Poke, a high-crowned, deep-brimmed hat, ca. 1840s.

Shawls, already in use for many years, remained an important part of most women's wardrobes, especially in the late 1840s and the 1850s. The typical shawl consisted simply of a large, square piece of material folded into a triangle and worn over the costume. The costliest, made of fine cashmere wool, sold in New York for $350, the same price as a small house. Paisley, similar in style but mass produced, was more affordable and extremely popular. Knitted shawls shared the lower end of the scale with those of homespun wool.

Jewelry became heavier. Sentimental pieces were widely worn, such as bracelets or brooches set with semiprecious stones. Exquisite pins featuring floral designs incorporated everything from the most precious gems to colored glass. Thanks to mass production, similar items were readily available and within reach of everyone but the most impoverished.

Fashionable shawl, ca. 1850–1860.

Throughout the 19th and into the 20th centuries, no lady left the house without a parasol, gloves, and a reticule. Ladies' parasols had come into general use during the late 18th century and were intended to protect the complexion, which had to be kept pale at all cost. White skin and soft hands were the marks of the leisured elite, as true gentility exhibited no visible sign of labor. Women of the increasingly vast middle class tried desperately to look like the upper classes, who took their hints directly from Paris. Freckles and suntan, which might imply hard work outdoors, were combatted with applications of bleaching buttermilk. Rouge, powder, and mascara were the signs of a "naughty" woman, since cosmetics were not used by proper ladies (although young ones might pinch their cheeks or brush them with red geranium petals to produce the suggestion of a blush). Hands were protected by gloves at all times, and roughness was treated with a liberal slathering of goose grease. Reticules—usually small drawstring sacks—carried the necessities: a handkerchief, a case with visiting cards, a purse with some money in it, and a vial of smelling salts to ward off faintness occasioned by tightly laced corsets but passed off as a blow to the sensibilities. A fan was an absolute necessity at a time when clothes were so tight and heavy that any exertion could bring on an unladylike sweat. It was also a useful tool for flirtatiously inclined girls, who kept the language of the fan alive.

In conservative areas like New England and remote areas like the frontier, fashion changes often lagged behind. The laboring classes could still afford few clothes, and their main concerns were warmth and decency. Many depended on hand-me-downs, and clothes were remade again and again. The least shabby pieces of material from several sources were combined to create one wearable garment. Shawls were often the only form of outerwear, and shoes remained a luxury in many parts of the country. But, however humble, a woman always wore a bonnet in public and a cap at home.

Death was a constant factor in women's lives. When it invaded a woman's family, she laid aside her usual clothes for mourning garments made in the current style. This custom continued well into the 20th century and was especially ritualized during and following the Civil War. It is important to note that a goodly portion of any woman's life was spent in mourning.

For women in the bereaved family, first or full mourning required unrelieved black. Second or half mourning called for gray, white, or shades of purple. All accessories were available in these colors.

A widow was expected to wear full mourning—only dull fabrics in black and trimmed with crepe—for an entire year. Even undergarments were trimmed in black, and white handkerchiefs were made with black borders that would be diminished as time passed. Whenever she left home, a widow's face was completely covered by a crepe veil. Unless they remarried, widows might wear black for the rest of their lives.

The death of a child or parent also required a full year of mourning, of a sibling or grandparent, six months. When full mourning was finished, another several months would be spent observing half mourning.

In addition to the mourning colors, pieces of hair from the dear departed were often woven and mounted in rings or brooches, to be worn in the later stages.

The Industrial Revolution, which began in England during the mid-18th century, changed textile manufacturing forever. In 1794, an American named Eli Whitney patented the cotton gin, a machine that quickly and easily removed the seeds from cotton blossoms. Mr. Whitney's invention ushered in mass production of cotton in the South, which made it readily available to mills in both the United States and Britain, who began producing cloth faster and in greater quantities than ever before. The invention of the sewing machine in the early 1850s and its subsequent adaptation for use in the home permitted increasing elaboration and diversity of styles, which began to change at a more rapid pace. With the replacement of people-powered machinery by steam-operated, home spinning and weaving became a thing of the past, and women were left with more time to concentrate on the form of what they wore.

Photography, introduced in the 1840s, brought the first objective records of what people wore. Engraved fashion plates had existed for years, but, like today's fashion magazines, they tended to depict only the most revolutionary, at times even ludicrous, styles.

Comparing photographs to fashion plates of the time points out the difference between reality and high fashion.

The great push westward began early in the 19th century, and women rode in covered wagons or walked alongside the men to help establish farmsteads in the wilderness. Simple, sturdy clothes were required. Gingham, calico, and other durable fabrics were turned into dresses with high necks, long sleeves, and full, gathered skirts which were worn over chemises and stays (even on the frontier these were seldom abandoned) as well as underdrawers and petticoats. The sunbonnet, a broad-brimmed head covering with a frill to shade the back of the neck and strings to secure it under the chin, derived directly from the poke bonnet and is visible

Pioneer woman, mid-19th century.

in photographs taken well into the 20th century. It not only protected the complexion from the sun, but also shaded the eyes from glare long before sun glasses were invented. Footwear usually took the form of sturdy boots, as it had to be equal to field work and long journeys afoot over rough terrain.

During this time, immigrants from various European nations poured into the United States, shedding their native costumes as soon as possible and merging, at least in appearance, into the mainstream.

Precursor of the sunbonnet, early 19th century.

Technology that came into use after the Civil War, including widely available electric power, directly affected the style and manufacture of clothing. In the early 1850s, commercial sewing machines enabled the large-scale manufacture of ready-to-wear apparel. However, the introduction of paper patterns for home dressmakers in the 1850s brought systematic sizes, making it easier and quicker to find a proper fit. Aniline and chemical dyes, perfected in the late 1850s, presented an entirely new palette of fashion colors. And, thanks to mail-order catalogues, women in even the remotest prairie settlements could avail themselves of well-made, sturdy, and fashionable clothing and accessories.

Between the Civil War and World War II, a succession of distinctly different silhouettes came and went. Hoops gave way to bustles, followed by a reprise of huge sleeves, and later the high-waisted "empire" line was revived, newly coupled with a tight, restricting skirt. Next came the so-called "flapper" style, and in the final decade of this period, women's clothes achieved the basic format that has lasted almost to the end of the 20th century.

Freed slave wearing turban, post-Civil War.

A woman's place remained in the home. Many women, however, encouraged by their newfound enfranchisement in 1920, began to enter professions. Within the rapidly burgeoning middle class, wives tended to their children and their increasingly comfortable homes. In the late 19th and early 20th centuries, wives and daughters of new millionaires took their money to Europe and stocked their wardrobes in Paris. Immigrants and other poor women, and often their children, sewed long hours in factories or at home on piecework for minimal wages. A good worker might earn $5.00 to $8.00 a week and find the blouse she had made for sale at prices between $2.69 and $12.49. Farm wives shared their husbands' grueling hours, often working in the fields in addition to raising the children, keeping house, and cooking for the entire farm population.

After the Civil War, many freed slaves continued to live on the plantations or farms of their former owners, sometimes working for wages and sometimes not. By and large their clothing did not change. Women covered their heads with cloth turbans, often made of brightly colored bandannas. Other blacks moved to towns or cities, where they were little better off than rural blacks, frequently relying on handed-down clothes. Blacks who made it to the middle class dressed accordingly.

Fullness in back of dress, late 1860s.

In the mid-1860s, the hoop slowly changed its shape from completely round to triangular. By the end of the decade, fullness had passed from the front of the female form to the back. The increasing masses of material at the back were supported by the bustle, an appendage made of wire and tape that tied around the waist and was designed to fold into itself when the wearer sat down. The bodice and skirt were usually made of the same fabric and trimmed in fabrics of contrasting shades. By now, chemical dyes were in general use, and colors ranged from pastel to violent.

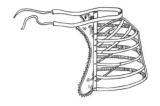

Bustle, 1888.

Throughout the 1870s, the bustle grew more and more elaborate as skirts diminished in breadth and lengthened into a train behind. Bodices grew longer and began to fit snugly over the hips in front. Corsets also grew longer, covering stomach and hips to produce a smooth, unbroken line. Necklines were generally high, often with frills at the throat, usually low-cut in evening gowns. Sleeves were long for both day and evening dress.

Train skirt and long bodice, 1875.

By the late 1870s, the original bustle had almost completely disappeared, only to return to fashion as large as ever with a modified, angular shape. The new bustle was accompanied by a severely tailored bodice that extended up to a high collar, except in formal wear.

As emphasis shifted to the back of the costume, it also moved to the back of the head. The smooth center part was abandoned and hair was swept away from the face to the crown, fully exposing ears for the first time in decades. A cascade of curls (supplemented when nature was remiss) fell down the back to the shoulders. Flat bonnets tilted forward, decorated with a profusion of flowers, feathers, ribbons, and lace trimming. In the 1880s, with the more severe bustle, hair was drawn into a bun above the nape of the neck; a frizzled fringe or carefully arranged spit curls might adorn the forehead. Tall shakos inspired by cylindrical military headgear of Hungarian origin were adopted, and bonnets almost completely disappeared.

Emphasis on back of costume, ca. 1880.

Prudery dictated that feet remain hidden. The accidental exposure of an ankle raised eyebrows at a time when evening dresses had deep decolletage. Unseen feet were encased in either ankle-high boots with elastic sides or low-cut, unlaced shoes.

Top: Flat bonnet profusely decorated, ca. 1875. Bottom: Shako, hat resembling military headgear, ca. 1885.

The newly exposed ears were adorned with long, pendant earrings. Lockets on chains or ribbons were popular, often containing photographs of loved ones. During the 1880s, "dog collars," wide ornamental necklaces (sometimes bejeweled) that covered the throat, were fashionable, a style that persisted for many years.

Dog collar necklace, ca. 1880–1890.

Photographs of novelist Edith Wharton and actress Lillian Russell show this accessory. A similar effect could be achieved by a wide ribbon with an ornament pinned to the front.

In 1890, the bustle withdrew altogether, although fullness at the back remained for some years. As skirts grew smaller, puffs or pleats began to appear, adding fullness at the shoulder. Sleeves gradually grew into a reprise of the huge sleeves of the 1830s. The hourglass figure with a pouter pigeon bosom and lushly spreading hips was every woman's target.

In spite of corsets, however, most women looked more like a cello than an hourglass. Necklines for daytime featured boned collars that reached to just under the chin. In the evening, bared bosoms adorned with elegant necklaces were standard.

In the 1890s, the "mauve decade," all shades of purple were very much in vogue. The prevailing fashion opinion stated that "too much is not enough," as one lady put it, and jewelry was worn in profusion. Both day and night, women were walking advertisements of their husband's wealth. Jeweled lorgnettes enabled them to see without resorting to glasses; eyestrain was often preferable to pince-nez. Discreetly applied cosmetics

Puffs and pleats appear, ca. 1890.

were acceptable, but obvious use of "paint" pointed to the stage or worse. A dusting of powder might serve to tame a shiny nose and a pale pink salve gave subtle color to the lips, but that was all. Complexions were still rigorously guarded from the sun by hats and parasols.

The years between 1860 and 1890 saw a lessening of doll-like helplessness as women started to contemplate the possibility of equality of the sexes. Thanks in part to labor-saving machinery in the home, women were participating in sports in numbers never before seen. A special outfit evolved

Hourglass figure and leg-of-mutton sleeves, ca. 1895.

for swimming, which had heretofore consisted of splashing helplessly in shallow water in a shapeless, tentlike garment. It was a knee-length dress over ankle-length trousers, stockings, and laced-up shoes, topped off by a bonnet. Wearing yards of material, women began to join men in croquet and, by the mid-1870s, the popular new game of tennis (for which the skirt might be shortened to ankle-length). While attending women's colleges, they did mild calisthenics in loose, knee-length skirts over ankle-length bloomers. In the 1890s, bicycling became the rage, and knee-length bloomers, minus hampering

Bicycling costume, ca. 1890s.

Left: Bathing suit, ca. 1890s. Right: Duster for motorist, ca. 1900.

skirts, provided freedom of movement along with modesty. These shorter bloomers were also worn for gymnastics and field sports, eventually showing up as part of the swimming costume, in the place of trousers. Stockings, usually made of heavy black cotton, were always worn with bloomers. With the advent of the automobile, motorists covered their clothes with long, unbleached linen overcoats called "dusters" and anchored their wide hats with veils to protect faces from the ravages of wind, dirt, and sun as they tore through the countryside at speeds of up to 30 miles per hour. The lack of windshields required that goggles be worn to protect the eyes.

The Gibson girl epitomized all that was most admired in American women in 1900. She was the "new woman" of the new century: tall, slim-waisted (achieved by her corset), wearing a high-necked, full-sleeved blouse or shirtwaist with a full, flowing skirt, her hair pinned up in a pompadour style. Here, as usual, the norm was often far from the ideal,

Gibson girl corset, ca. 1900s.

Top: Gibson girl with pompadour, ca. 1900s. Bottom: Working girl in bolero jacket, ca. 1905.

and when gravity had its way and loose ends stuck out, the pompadour became rather untidy. Those unfortunates whose tresses were not thick enough to achieve the desired look arranged their hair over pads called "rats" to supplement their supply. Hats became broad brimmed and often overladen with imitation fruits, flowers, and occasionally entire birds. Many women more sensibly adopted the straw "boater" for informal wear.

Around this time, more women began to enter the office as "typewriters," espousing the Gibson girl blouse and skirt as efficient and businesslike attire. A short bolero jacket worn over the blouse and a hat, gloves, and handbag completed the working girl's outfit. To enhance what was known as the "Grecian bend," corsets thrust the bosom forward and the posterior backward, giving the body an "S" curve.

By now footwear was largely mass-produced rather than hand-cobbled and was available in standardized sizes. The medium- or high-heeled, calf-covering, high-button shoe is most often associated with this period, but lower-cut, laced shoes were worn in the daytime. For evening dress, pumps with fabric bows or jeweled buckles held sway.

The silhouette had changed again by 1910. Skirts became shorter and tighter until the "hobble skirt" had to be split for easy walking. When the skirt reached as high as the ankles, it was covered by a mid-calf overskirt. Getting in and out of streetcars and other conveyances in a hobble skirt was extremely awkward. Waistlines rose and began to be defined with a wide belt or sash below the bustline in emulation of the empire style. For evening wear,

"Grecian bend" gives body "S" curve, ca. 1905.

bodices were softly draped; chiffon, which lent itself to this style, was often used. Echoing the latest look in outer wear, corsets also grew shorter above the natural waistline and longer below it, reaching nearly to the knees as they had a century before. Sitting down was a challenge. Under the corset, women still wore chemises, which had dwindled to mere wisps, and knee-length drawers with open crotches. Petticoats hung from the waist. Stockings were held up by snap garters attached to the corset. Shoes with pointed toes and high, curved "Louis" heels (named after a popu-

Corset used under straight skirt, ca. 1911.

lar mid-18th-century French design), were often teamed with spats—short gaiters that covered the ankles. High boots, laced or buttoned, as well as low-cut pumps, are prevalent in contemporary photographs. Hats, worn over modified pompadours, were very wide and held in place by long hatpins, handy tools for discouraging mashers from taking liberties with unescorted women.

Large hat with veil and feathers, ca. 1910.

Fur and feather boas were the usual accessories, along with large muffs. Gloves, parasols, and reticules, by now distinctly handbags, remained in use. No lady left the house without gloves. In the evening they were long and white, and tight enough to outline the fingernails. As hats became larger, parasols went out of style. Fans, often made of feathers, remained a part of the evening ensemble after the turn of the century.

The war that broke out in Europe in 1914 had a great influence on American designs. A jaunty military appearance was considered chic, hemlines rose, and waistlines began to lower. Hats became smaller and tighter fitting, and hair dressed more closely to the head. Some women even joined the armed forces when the United States entered the war in 1917. Their uniforms were a mishmash of current styles wedded to military clothes. Army women wore ankle-length skirts topped by tailored khaki jackets similar to the male soldiers'. Feet were shod in laced, calf-high boots, heads adorned with a campaign hat. The navy's "yeomanette" uniform was a blue tunic and ankle-length skirt, laced boots, and a nautically styled hat.

On the home front, more and more women entered the workplace to substitute for men in the military. In factories, shops, and offices, women found that a more active lifestyle demanded freedom of movement and correspondingly less cumbersome clothing. Never again in this century would hemlines reach to the ground except for formal or home wear.

Another war casualty of even more importance was extreme prudery. With the arrival of shorter skirts and greater quantities of exposed legs, both "limbs" and exposed flesh began to lose their capacity to shock. With less cumbersome clothes, women could participate more actively in social sports, which led to the acknowledgment, albeit indirectly, of female perspiration. In *Vogue* Magazine of February 9, 1916, an advertisement claims that the new "Mum ... greatly neutralizes all bodily odors." Even corseting relented somewhat; in the same magazine Lane Bryant offers "Maternity Corsets" that "preserve health of mother and child; harmonize figure lines throughout the entire period; prevent clothes from binding."

Left: Military-inspired civilian clothing, ca. 1917.
Right: WWI Marinette uniform, ca. 1917.

By 1920, waistlines had paused briefly at the natural position, then continued to descend while hemlines were rising. Curves disappeared as objects of admiration, and by 1924, the "flapper" reigned supreme. Although this bosomless, hipless hoyden has often been used to characterize an entire decade, she actually only held sway for about four years. Most women were simply unable to achieve the desired effect, no matter how hard they tried.

The distinctly separate bodice and skirt of old was completely gone. The new silhouette was a sheath dress or a skirt and loose overblouse, with arms fully exposed for the first time. Elaborate beading and expensive fabrics, exhibited by designers in New York, were imitated in less expensive materials by many a woman in her home sewing room.

Beaded dress, early 1920s.

To affect the boyish look, women wore forerunners of the bra called bandeaux to flatten their breasts and compressed their hips and buttocks in a girdle made of knitted elastic. Underdrawers shortened to above the knee, and the petticoat was replaced by a slip.

Flapper sheath dress and cloche hat, ca. 1924.

Corset, 1928.

The standard chemise disappeared altogether. Sheer stockings (rolled to below the knees by the very young) covered newly exposed legs. Shoes had high heels and pointed toes.

Immediately after the war and for the next several years, hairstyles were soft around the face with a knot of curls at the back, but during the war many women had their hair "bobbed" and found short styles easier to live with. Hair was often set in tightly crimped waves called "marcels." The permanent wave was introduced to Europe in 1906 and soon came to the United States, but took hours to accomplish and was extremely expensive. By the 1920s, when the most stylish had carried bobbing a step further, exposing both ears and nape, the permanent had found wider use. True flappers wore their hair very short and straight to look as boyish as possible.

Boyish bob, ca. 1920s.

It wasn't until the 1920s, primarily as a result of the conspicuous use of makeup in movies, that women openly began to use cosmetics. Foundation cream, face powder, lipstick, rouge, eyebrow pencil, mascara, and eye shadow came into common use. Eyebrows were plucked to a thin, high arch, and lips fashioned into the "bee sting," a pouty look popularized by Clara Bow, the reigning sex symbol of that period. Colored nail polish, available in a variety of garish shades, arrived in the late 1920s.

Matching jacket and skirt, mid-1930s.

Post-World War I hats generally had fairly wide brims and deep crowns. As the amount of hair diminished, so did the hat. The tight-fitting, brimless cloche was the most suitable accompaniment to the flapper's bobbed hair. Jewelry adapted also; long necklaces hung well below the breasts, and dangling earrings counterbalanced the boyish form. Several bangle bracelets might be worn on each wrist.

By now, cleanliness was taken for granted. Daily baths or showers and deodorants were considered necessities, women shaved their legs and their armpits, and a clean, wholesome, casual look (the "all-American girl") was predominant.

Hollywood and the technicolor movies being produced in the 1930s were responsible for many of the popular styles of dress. Some Hollywood costume designers, most notably Adrian, were recruited by the garment industry. Mass production of these designs enabled star-struck girls to wear the same glamorous apparel as their favorite actresses. Parisian fashions served as another foundation for popular trends, as American designers had for years adapted and redefined them for domestic tastes.

The stock-market crash of 1929 had a profound effect on American clothes. Many people could no longer afford to follow the latest fads and fancies of New York fashion and became correspondingly careful about spending money on what they wore. Clothing became more practical, with simpler and sturdier fabrics chosen over what had been favorites a few years earlier.

In the years between the crash and the beginning of World War II, the straight-line, boyish look gave way to soft curves. As waistlines once again rose, hemlines fell. Dresses cut on the bias emphasized movement and the body's shape. Chanel, whose designs epitomize this period, often used jersey for dressmaking. She was one of the first to employ a fabric called "artificial silk," which today is known as rayon. Day dresses ended at mid-calf, while evening skirts were floor length. A waist-length jacket and matching skirt with a separate blouse became standard wear. Toward the end of the 1930s, shoulder padding came into style, accompanied by severe tailoring. The introduction of the zipper opened new possibilities in clothing style and design.

For the first time, so-called "beach pajamas," or trousers with wide legs, were worn by women in public, first appearing at seaside resorts and in California. The appearance of Greta Garbo and other movie stars in tailored slacks opened the way for the wholesale adoption of pants and, eventually, shorts. Blue jeans, hitherto worn only by farmers and cowboys, had found places in the wardrobes of some venturesome young women by the late 1930s.

The modern bra was developed when breasts and hips were released from constricting corsets and the bandeaux of the

Beach pajamas, late 1930s.

1920s were discarded. By the mid-1930s, the bra had been successfully engineered to support the breasts. Panties now had crotches and were worn over girdles; they had become formfitting or very short with flared legs. Real or artificial silk was used for underwear, and pastel shades were popular. Silk or cotton stockings were fashioned in natural colors, with seams that ran down the back of the leg.

As hemlines got longer, hair followed suit. It was usually brushed to one side with a full wave and curls below the earlobes. While women had "helped" their hair for centuries, it was not until the actress Jean Harlow popularized platinum blonde that women hit the bleach bottle en masse. Eyebrows remained ultra thin well into the 1930s, only gradually moving toward a more natural appearance, as did the shape of the mouth. Cosmetic colors became considerably softer. If a naturally acquired suntan (now considered healthy looking) was not possible, makeup would provide it.

Low-back bathing suit, ca. 1930s.

Small hats came with veils and tilted forward on one side of the head. Women continued to wear gloves and carry purses, but muffs were no longer a must. Costume jewelry came into fashion; even those who could afford the real thing enjoyed the variety that costume jewelry made readily available.

Large collars and wide cuffs of fur began to appear as coat trimmings. Silver fox lent itself well to this fashion. A stole fashioned from a pair of small animal skins, joined together with the head of

Tennis sportswear, ca. 1930s.

one clamped to the feet of the other, was considered especially elegant with suits and overcoats.

With greater freedom of movement and less false modesty, 20th-century maternity wear evolved into a loose smock worn over an expandable skirt. Tightly laced corsets had disappeared in the 1920s, but doctors still advocated the use of a garment that gave some support to the back and cradled the stomach. Physical activity during pregnancy was curtailed, and in the final stages women were encouraged not to travel too far from home.

Sportswear constituted an ever increasing portion of most women's wardrobes. Bathing costumes lost their bloomers, then their sleeves, and lastly their stockings to become one-piece, formfitting tank suits, abbreviations that were cut low in the back and often in the front as well. Short, pleated skirts with matching underpants appeared on tennis courts, where stockings were abandoned in favor of socks. Clothing designed expressly for skating, skiing, golfing, sailing, hiking, and other physical activities could be found in all price ranges.

WAVES Navy uniform, ca. 1940s.

In the 50 years between World War II and 1990, many changes took place in women's lives and in their clothing. World War II, the Vietnam War, agitation for civil and women's rights, and the space age all had a direct impact on how people dressed. Technologies developed during this period led to new synthetic fabrics as well as the almost complete mechanization of clothing production, which made all styles immediately available in a great range of prices.

During World War II, instead of adapting men's uniforms for wo-men in the armed forces, American designers created uniforms that reflected current female styles. Jackets (tunics) were worn over shirts with neckties, and skirts ended just below the knee. WACs, army women, wore olive-drab tunics and skirts, beige cotton shirts and ties, and brown leather gloves and shoes. WAVES, the naval equivalent, wore navy blue uniforms with white shirts, blue scarves, black leather shoes, and white gloves. In summer, the entire WAVE uniform was white. The Women's Marine Corps wore a similar outfit in olive green. Nylon stockings, unobtainable by civilians because the material

WWII factory worker in tunic and pants, ca. 1940s.

was needed for military purposes, were issued to women in all branches. Nurses and other active duty personnel wore pants, as did women in factory jobs and on farms.

During the wartime years, it was American designers, rather than European, who determined what was worn by American women. Inspired by the Spanish and Native American heritage in the Southwest, they offered low-cut, frilled-neck blouses, tiered skirts, and silver jewelry set with turquoises. The geometric designs and earth colors used in Native American rugs and blankets were adapted to fabrics. The shirtdress proved an all-purpose garment that could be dressed up or down according to need. Among the innovators was Clare McCardell, who first introduced "separates," ensembles of interchangeable skirts and blouses. Clothing styles reflected wartime fabric shortages and the need for practicality; skirts became shorter, stopping just below the knee. Large shoulder pads lent a military air to jackets and coats and were used in dresses as well. This rather stern outline was softened by ruffles, peplums, and extremely elegant hats.

Hair was swept up in front and worn in a modified pompadour

Southwestern influence, early 1940s.

Knee-length dress and elaborate hat, ca. 1940s.

with a curled under "pageboy" style in back. Factory women bundled their hair into heavy snoods and wore bandannas over their heads for safety and cleanliness.

Because leather was rationed, shoes had to be made of canvas or synthetic fabrics. With silk and nylon unavailable for civilian use, women wore rayon or cotton stockings or "painted" their legs with a washable dye. As seamless stockings were still unheard of, eyebrow pencil was often used to create a more realistic look. "Bobby sox," heavy white socks rolled down to the ankles, were worn with loafers or saddle shoes.

Wartime gloves were made of cotton rather than leather. Purses became larger to accommodate the increased store of necessities women carried with them—makeup, cigarettes, handkerchiefs, car keys, wallets. The convenient shoulder bag appeared and has persisted.

The late 1940s saw two major advances. First, the swimsuit of earlier decades underwent a radical change with the introduction of the bikini (which seems modest in comparison to what is worn now). Second, pregnancy evolved from a shame to be concealed

Early bikini, late 1940s.

to a condition to be endured, or even enjoyed, in comfort. Dresses appeared on the market that were designed specifically for expectant women, with elasticized sides that allowed the figure to expand naturally. Maternity skirts had adjustable panels and were worn with overblouses.

In complete revolt against wartime austerity, Christian Dior introduced the "New Look" in the fall of 1947. It was a curvy, utterly feminine look and an immediate hit. Shoulders diminished and became softly rounded, and a tiny waist (often helped with a "cinch") was complemented by a full skirt that reached almost to the ankles. The hardy, perennial shirtdress of the 1940s lasted for sev-

"New Look" of diminished shoulders and full skirt, 1947.

eral decades, its hemline rising or falling, and its fit tight or loose in accordance with current styles. Adaptations appeared all over the country. Strapless, full-length evening gowns were worn over hooped petticoats. This style has disappeared and reappeared several times, becoming a veritable fixture among Southern girls elected to serve as queens and princesses of festivals, homecomings, and parades of all sorts.

Shirtdress, ca. 1950s.

Shoes of the late 1940s had platform heels and ankle straps. Nylon, released from wartime rationing, began to be used for stockings and underwear, soon finding its way into blouses and dresses. Tight choker necklaces, scarab and charm bracelets, and lapel pins were the favorite items of jewelry.

A complete turnaround took place in the early 1950s with the appearance of the "sack" dress, harkening back to the 1920s with its simpler, straighter line that emphasized the body's movement and threw out Dior's New Look. The 1954 A-line had a slightly higher waistline and was often sleeveless. In the late 1950s, as hemlines began to creep up again, the trapeze, a pyramid shape (another Dior innovation) caught on, a style that adapted readily to maternity wear.

In the early 1950s, hairdressers began using "cold" permanent waves, which did not require the cumbersome machinery of the older version and shortened the time required to perform the operation. Shortly thereafter home perms appeared. A new hairdressing tool, the roller,

Sleeveless sack dress, ca. 1950s.

which allowed looser curls, came on the market in 1958. Ornamented bandeaux with veils, feather caps, or berets took the place of elaborate millinery.

The ballet shoe, a soft-soled, flat-heeled slipper, replaced platform shoes as standard footwear. At the end of the 1950s, extremely high, stiletto spike heels and pointed toes came into vogue and remained into the next decade. They were very uncomfortable and harmful to hardwood floors, but no woman considered herself well dressed without them.

Heavy eyebrows were back in style and with them long (often fake) eyelashes and eyeliner began to appear on eyelids and under the eye. Liquid makeup replaced pancake, which had to be applied with a sponge, and blushers replaced rouge.

With the A-line, longer necklaces came back, and earrings, both large and small, were popular. Costume and plastic "junk" jewelry was popular at every social level. Experiments with synthetic material brought various fake or "fun" furs into use.

The 1960s was a period of confusion and contradictory outlooks that affected clothing styles. Television, by now in almost every home, brought events and styles directly into people's lives. The Vietnam War had a divisive effect and contributed to a strong movement among the young for peace among nations and generations. The long flowing garments, loose hair, and "love beads" of beatniks, flower children, and hippies, reflected their rebellion against their parents' styles and ideas. Most women noted with interest what the soap-opera and situation-comedy heroines wore. The popularity of astronauts

Hippy, late 1960s, early 1970s.

Pillbox hat and boxy jacket, ca. 1960.

and space exploration encouraged designers to promote streamlined styles and synthetic materials in everything from hats to shoes.

Hemlines began to inch upwards. Form-fitting sheath dresses or skirts with boxy jackets that brushed the hips were fashionable. The "beehive" hairdo, a back-combed, lacquered, and sprayed concoction not unlike the "heads" of the 18th century, lingered for many years, but most women preferred a looser style. In the early 1960s, Jackie Kennedy popularized the large pillbox hat worn at the back of the head. Nothing was ever devised to cover the beehive.

In the late 1960s, the miniskirt brought hemlines up to mid-thigh and put more emphasis on legs. The extreme mini looked dated after a few years and got a little bit longer, to the relief of those who worried about indecent exposure. The pantsuit of matching jacket and tailored pants appeared alongside the mini, perhaps for women who disliked showing so much leg. Perhaps the greatest and most lasting blessing brought about by the mini was pantyhose. The mini's successor, the ankle-length maxi-skirt, was short-lived.

Extreme mini, late 1960s.

During the 1960s, the civil rights movement fostered a new awareness of African American heritage, and ethnic pride was expressed in fashion. Alex Haley's "Roots" inspired many black women to choose clothing derived from African dress, which featured vibrant colors and striking patterns.

Hair was often plaited in many tight braids arranged in decorative designs, which took a long time to create and might be left in place for days. The "Afro," in which hair was brushed out at a uniform length all around the head, was another popular choice for African Americans. The overall effect was complemented by jewelry crafted to look like traditional African pieces.

Throughout this same period the women's movement blossomed and grew. The most ardent feminists burned their bras, which they felt symbolized the oppression of the white male power structure. Some women activists adopted an androgynous look or expressed their displeasure with the status quo by ignoring fashion completely.

African-influenced dress, ca. 1970s.

The 1970s reacted to the dichotomies of the previous decade with conspicuous consumption of all consumer goods, including clothes. In this decade, women's increasing demand for equality manifested itself in "unisex" clothing. At times it was hard to tell the boys from the girls: both wore blue jeans, T-shirts, and long hair.

Early in the decade, hems came down again, and more and more women regularly wore pants. Polyesters, including Lycra and similar formfitting fabrics, came into wide use, especially in so-called "stretch" pants. T-shirts, which started life as men's underwear, were worn everywhere. At first, women wore jeans made for men or boys, which were not always comfortable; then manufacturers began tailoring jeans specifically for women. During the late 1960s and early 1970s, these often had flared legs. Stiff, unyielding denims were made pliable by "stone washing," a process that softened as well as faded the jeans to a soft blue. The fit improved with the use of stretch fabrics.

Denim jeans and T-shirt, ca. 1970s.

Hairstyles loosened up and hair color began to be enhanced by "streaking"—adding highlighted strands to the natural shade—or even by changing the color completely. Boots, worn heretofore only outside as foul weather protection, came indoors and appeared in soft, pliable materials. Fabrics developed for use in space turned out to be well adapted for sportswear. Lightweight but durable, some of them were especially suited for ski or swim wear.

Tailored suit and blouse of career woman, ca. 1970s.

Women were offered more options and greater flexibility in their choice of clothing, but suitability to the occasion remained an important factor. Career women wore outfits that almost looked like uniforms; tailored suits with blouses that often had a high neckline tied in a bow. Many women continued to work during pregnancy, and maternity wear began to follow current fashion. By the 1990s, the pregnant woman could find everything from exercise wear to evening dresses in all the latest colors, fabrics, and styles made expressly for her needs.

During the 1980s, a dizzying succession of clothing styles appeared that combined various elements from earlier fashions. Nostalgia seemed to be the primary motif in designs that revived and updated looks from the 1920s, 1930s, 1940s, and even the 1950s and 1960s. Natural fabrics, such as linen and silk, supplanted polyesters in the most expensive clothes. Hemlines descended to the ankles, and long, full skirts re-

Career woman, ca. 1980s.

called the New Look of the late 1940s. Short, slim skirts climbed above the knees very much like the mini of the 1960s. Shoulders got broader in a replay of the wartime 1940s look, then diminished. High waistlines were borrowed from the A-line of the 1950s, and low waistlines harkened back to the flapper era. The bias-cut dresses

Layered look, ca. 1980s.

of the 1930s were recreated with modern fabrics. The "layered" look of sweaters or vests worn over turtleneck jerseys was popular and went equally well with both skirts and pants. By 1990, skirts were knee-length or above, but shoulders remained broad.

As physical fitness became more of a national obsession, exercise clothes, from baggy sweatpants and sweatshirts to body-hugging leotards, appeared everywhere. The desire for a trim, slender body had women of all ages trying diets coupled with aerobic exercise routines. Aware that overexposure to the sun could cause skin cancer, women no longer tried to achieve deep tans, and makeup shades became correspondingly paler. In the late 1980s, heavy eyebrows and pouty lips made a comeback. While many chose to wear their hair long, either loose or frizzled, others preferred a short style that echoed the 1920s boyish bob. Large-brimmed hats reappeared. Long, dangling earrings, multiple strand necklaces, rings on several fingers, and chunky bracelets were in style. Colored or opaque stockings were worn with narrow-heeled shoes, and many women wore jogging shoes

Sweatsuit, ca. 1980–1990.

Practical, modern dress, ca. 1990.

with tailored suits on their way to or from work.

It would seem that the old maxim "never throw anything away" can be applied to one's wardrobe. Although it is not safe to predict what fashion will someday decree, hoopskirts, bustles, and floor-length skirts are probably gone forever from everyday use. Fashion designers will continue to introduce new lines, or variations of old ones, and display them on fashion models who represent some aesthetic ideal of female beauty. Computers already help to redesign and to retool the clothing industry for an increasingly rapid turnover of styles. As in the past, most women will keep their eyes on the styles, but dress rather differently. A few will try to emulate the latest fashions, but most will probably adapt what they feel is appropriate for their life-styles and dress themselves in what they see as most becoming, practical, and suitable.

Because of its fragility, much early clothing is kept in storage where it can be examined by serious students. Museums and historical societies all over the United States have collections, and often some clothes are put on display in settings appropriate to their period. If you are interested in items not currently on display, it is customary to inquire with the museum curator to find out if an appointment to view the clothing might be possible.

Guides and interpreters at many historic sites wear historically accurate reproductions of period clothing, and offer the added advantage of a glimpse of the daily lives of the people who wore them. Again, inquiries should be made with the directors of such exhibits for more information.

Excellent costume books are available, and most libraries have some reference material on the subject. Books on American art, the history of photography, or period magazines and catalogues are all excellent sources of study. Current books in the field of social studies offer interpretations of clothing in the context of everyday life. Ask your local librarian for assistance.

The information in this book was drawn from many sources. The author relied, as much as possible, on material contemporary to the periods discussed. The following books are offered for the student who wishes to delve deeper into the subject of American dress than the constraints of this survey have allowed. It is not a complete bibliography.

Fisher, David Hacket. *Albion's Seed.* New York: Oxford University Press, 1989.

Green, Harvey. *The Light of the Home.* New York: Pantheon Books, 1983.

Kasson, John F. *Rudeness and Civility.* New York: Hill & Wang, 1990.

McClellan, Elisabeth. *History of American Costume.* New York: Tudor Publishing Company, 1904.

Milbank, Caroline Reynolds. *New York Fashion.* New York: Harry N. Abrams, Inc., 1989.

Smith, Barbara Clark and Peiss, Kathy. *Men and Women: A History of Costume, Gender and Power.* Washington, D.C.: Smithsonian Institution, 1989.

Spruill, Julia Cherry. *Women's Life and Work in the Southern Colonies.* New York: W. W. Norton & Co., 1938.

A-line A sleeveless dress with a high waistline.

bandeaux A strip of fabric worn over the chemise to flatten or hold the bosom firm.

boater A man's stiff, straw hat with a flat crown, ribbon band, and straight brim.

bobby sox A sock reaching above the ankle usually worn by teenage girls and children, typically with loafers or saddle shoes.

bloomers A costume for women introduced about 1850 consisting of a short skirt and long, loose trousers that are gathered closely at the knees forming a ruffle.

bombazine A twilled fabric with silk warp and worsted filling that is dyed various colors or black for mourning wear.

boned stays Long pins of whalebone or carved ivory that are inserted into the vertical pockets of a corset to help cinch the stomach and waist.

bustle A framework (as of whalebone, metal, crinoline) or a padded cushion that expands and supports the fullness and drapery of the back of a woman's skirt.

calash A large hood made on an arrangement of hoops to permit folding far back on the head.

camlet A European imitation of a medieval Asiatic fabric of camel's hair or Angora wool in a plain weave usually dyed a bright red.

chatelaine An ornamental chain, pin, or clasp usually worn at a woman's waist to which trinkets, keys, a purse, or other articles are attached.

chemise A woman's loose, shirtlike undergarment.

chiffon A sheer, plain-weave, light-weight fabric made of hard-twisted single yarns of wool, silk, cotton, rayon, or nylon and usually given a soft, dull finish.

cloche A woman's small, helmetlike hat usually with a deep, rounded crown and very narrow brim.

clogs A heavy shoe, sandal, or overshoe having a thick wooden sole.

commode A woman's cap made of lace, fine fabric, and ribbons over a high wire framework.

corset A woman's close-fitting, bone-stiffened, supporting undergarment often hooked and laced, extending from above or beneath the bust or from the waist to below the hips, and having garters attached.

crinoline A stiffened, open-weave fabric of horsehair or cotton used for interlining, and for underskirts to expand the overskirts.

dog collar A wide, flexible necklace composed of multiple rows of gems or beads that fits the neck snugly.

drugget A fabric made of wool or wool mixed with linen or silk formerly used for clothing.

duster A light-weight, washable overgarment usually made like a coat and worn to prevent clothing from becoming soiled.

"Empire" waistline A short-waisted dress pulled tight across the front and fastened at the sides or back with boned stays or pins.

farthingale A support made of hoops or a padded role worn beneath a skirt to swell out and extend it at the hip line.

fashion plate An illustration of a clothing style.

flax A slender annual that is widely cultivated for its long, silky bast fibers which when freed from the stem by retting and mechanical processes becomes the source of linen.

fustian A strong cotton and linen fabric used for clothing and bedding.

kersey A coarse-ribbed, woolen cloth for hose and work clothes woven first in medieval England.

linsey-woolsey A coarse, sturdy fabric with cotton warp and woolen filling.

"Louis" heel A French heel usually two inches or less in height.

lorgnettes A pair of eyeglasses or opera glasses with a handle.

lutestring A plain, glossy silk formerly used for women's dresses and ribbons.

mantle A very short cape or cloak.

padusoy A rich, heavy, corded silk fabric for clothing and upholstery.

paisley A colorful elaborate design made of a soft wool or similar material and consisting typically of curved abstract figures imitating East Indian patterns.

panniers A pair of hoops (made of steel or whalebone) formerly used to expand women's skirts at the sides.

pantalettes Long drawers having an attached or detachable ruffle at the bottom of each leg usually showing below the skirt and worn by women and children.

patten A clog, sandal, or overshoe often with a wooden sole or metal device to elevate the foot and increase the wearer's height or aid in walking through mud.

pelisse A long cloak or coat made of fur or lined or trimmed with fur and worn by men and women.

peplum A short, skirtlike section attached to the waistline of a blouse, jacket, or dress, and made usually with a flared, pleated, or ruffled design.

petticoat A skirt on its own waistband that is usually a little shorter than outer clothing and is often made with a ruffled, pleated, or lace edge.

pillbox hat A woman's small, round hat.

pince-nez Eyeglasses clipped to the nose by a wire spring.

poke A projecting brim on the front of a woman's bonnet.

reticule A woman's small, drawstring bag used as a pocketbook, workbag, or carryall.

sack dress (see Watteau sacque)

serge A durable, twilled fabric having a smooth, clear face and a pronounced diagonal rib on the front and on the back, made in various weights from worsted wool, cotton, silk, or rayon, and used especially for suits, coats, or dresses.

shift (see chemise)

smock (see chemise)

spats A covering for the instep and ankle usually made of cloth or leather with a side closing and a strap under the instep.

trapeze A short dress in the shape of a pyramid often used for maternity wear.

turban A woman's brimless, close-fitting hat of draped fabric.

wasp waist A woman's tightly laced waistline.

Watteau sacque A loosely fitting dress having back pleats falling from the neckline to the hem.

African Americans, 22, 38, 61
A-line, 58
apron, 11, 20
bandeaux, 48
bathing suit, 42, 43, 53, 56
beatnik, 59
beauty spot, 20
bikini, 56
bloomers, 30-31, 42
blue jeans, 51, 62
boa, 46
bobby sox, 56
bodice, 13, 15, 18, 24, 39
bra, 51-52, 61
bridal gown, 12
bustle, 37, 38-39, 41
calash, 19, 20
Chanel, 51
chatelaine, 21
chemise, 8, 15, 26, 45, 49
cloche, 50
commode, 15
corset, 16, 17, 25-26, 27, 31, 39, 44,
    45, 47
cosmetics, 10, 20-21, 24, 27, 29, 33,
    41-42, 49, 59, 64
Dior, Christian, 57, 58
duster, 43
empire waist, 25, 26, 37, 45
fabric, 12, 21, 22, 24, 36, 51, 58, 62
fan, 20, 34, 46
flapper, 48
Gibson girl, 43-44
hair styles, 8, 13, 15, 19, 20, 24, 26, 28,
    32, 39-40, 43-44, 49, 52, 55-56,
    58, 60, 61, 62, 64
hats, 8, 11, 18, 24, 26, 28, 32, 40, 44,
    46, 50, 52, 60, 64
hobble skirt, 45
hoop skirt, 29-30, 38
jewelry, 13, 21, 33, 40, 41, 50, 52, 64
layered look, 64

leg-of-mutton sleeve, 28
lorgnette, 41
mask, 8
maternity wear, 17, 22-23, 27, 28-29,
    53, 57, 58, 63
McCardell, Clare, 55
military uniform, 46, 54
miniskirt, 60
mourning, 23, 34-35
muff, 9, 46
pannier, 17
pants, 51, 55, 62
pantsuit, 60
parasol, 33
petticoat, 28, 29, 45, 48
pillbox hat, 60
pleats, 41
poke, 32, 36
Puritans, 10, 11, 12
purse, 56
Quakers, 14
reticule, 34, 46
round gown, 24
ruff, 9, 10
separates, 55
shako, 40
shawl, 32
sheath, 48
shift (see chemise)
shirtdress, 57
shoes, 9, 11, 18, 19, 26, 31, 36, 40, 44,
    45-46, 49, 58, 59, 62
snood, 32
Southern colonies, 8, 9, 21
Southwest style, 55
spats, 46
sportswear, 42-43, 53, 64
suit, 63
sunbonnet, 36
WAC, 54
Watteau sacque, 16, 20
WAVE, 54

"In olden days a glimpse of stocking was looked on as something shocking, Now, Goodness knows, anything goes." —Cole Porter, "Anything Goes"

"Fashion is a form of ugliness so intolerable that we have to alter it every six months." —Oscar Wilde

"Fashion: a despot whom the wise ridicule and obey." —Ambrose Bierce

"Every generation laughs at the old fashions, but follows religiously the new." —Henry David Thoreau

"Beware of all enterprises that require new clothes." —Henry David Thoreau

"There is not so variable a thing in nature as a lady's headdress." —Joseph Addison

"Her hat is a creation that will never go out of style; it will just look ridiculous year after year." —Fred Allen

"She was what we used to call a suicide blonde—dyed by her own hand." —Saul Bellow on Jean Harlow

"The jean! The jean is the destructor! It is a dictater! It is destroying creativity. The jean must be stopped." —Pierre Cardin, *People*, 1976

"Fashion exists for women with no taste, etiquette for people with no breeding." —Queen Marie of Romania